WHAT WILL YOU DRAW TODAY?

101 DRAWING PROMPTS WITH QUOTES

BY GLENYS MEE

THIS BOOK IS INTENDED TO BE DRAWN IN, SCRIBBLED
ON, AND SHOULD END UP DOG-EARED AND WELL USED!
EXTENDED IDEA: TAKE YOUR DRAWINGS FROM HERE
AND PAINT THEM! PLEASE TAKE PICTURES OF YOUR ART
AND EMAIL ME YOUR INTERPRETATIONS! I WOULD LOVE
TO SEE THEM!

glenysmee@mail.com
HAVE FUN!

DRAW ME! (EVEN THOUGH YOU'VE NEVER MET ME)

Draw the view from this window.

A morning-glory
at my window
satisfies me more than
the metaphysics
of books.

~Walt Whitman

DRAW A DOORKNOB.

(MY BROTHER USED TO LAUGH AT THEM AS A BABY.)

DRAW SOME SEASHELLS OF DIFFERENT SHAPES AND SIZES.

DRAW A STAIRWAY. WHERE DOES IT LEAD?

LIFE IS A SERIES OF STEPS. THINGS ARE DONE GRADUALLY.
ONCE IN A WHILE THERE IS A GIANT STEP,
BUT MOST OF THE TIME WE ARE TAKING SMALL,
SEEMINGLY INSIGNIFICANT STEPS ON THE STAIRWAY OF LIFE.

~RALPH RANSOM

Draw a feather.

Draw a comic in the boxes below. It doesn't have to be funny!

Draw a steaming hot cup of coffee or tea.

I HAVE MEASURED OUT
MY LIFE WITH COFFEE SPOONS.
~T. S. ELIOT

Draw a map of your house or town or state.
What would you change if you could?

DRAW A FAVORITE STUFFED ANIMAL. DO YOU STILL HAVE IT?

MINE IS A BEAR FROM A BELOVED AUNT, AND YES, I STILL HAVE IT!

DRAW TWO PEOPLE HUGGING.

I WILL NOT PLAY TUG O' WAR. I'D RATHER PLAY HUG O' WAR.
WHERE EVERYONE HUGS INSTEAD OF TUGS,
WHERE EVERYONE GIGGLES AND ROLLS ON THE RUG,
WHERE EVERYONE KISSES, AND EVERYONE GRINS,
AND EVERYONE CUDDLES, AND EVERYONE WINS.

~SHEL SILVERSTEIN

draw a building that you'd see on another planet, or in the future.

Draw a glass of water.

Where does the light hit the water and the glass?

DRAW A MANDALA. Mandala /ˈmændələ; mænˈdɑːlə/

noun (Hindu & Buddhist art) any of various designs symbolizing the universe, usually circular. (make symmetric patterns in and around the circle)

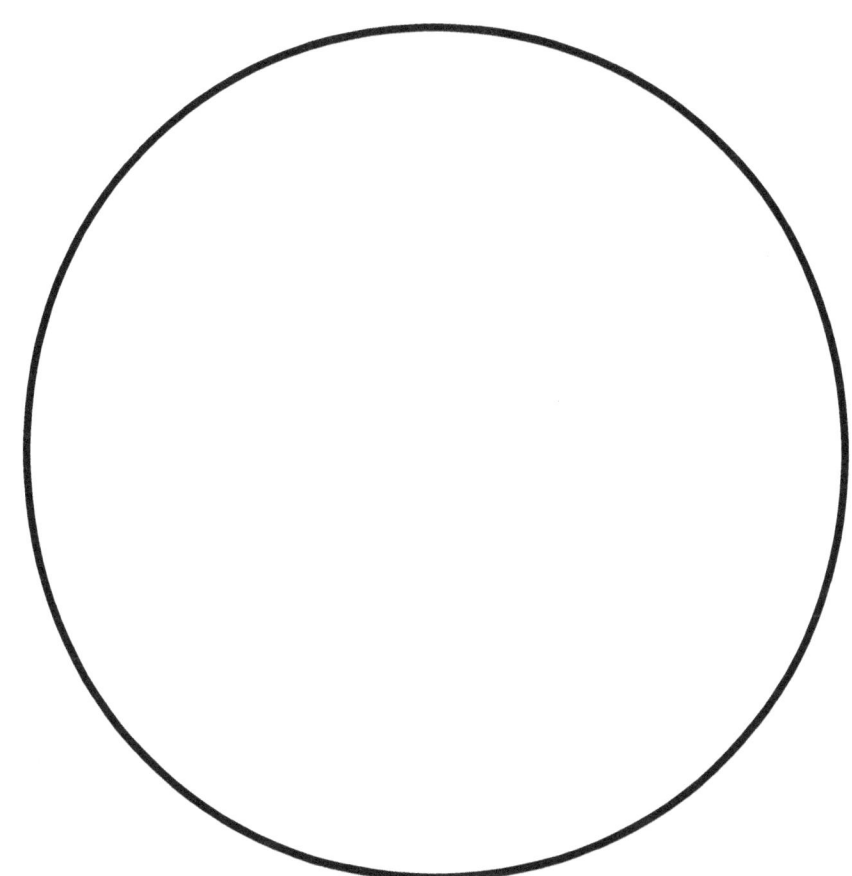

THE UNIVERSE IS BUILT ON A PLAN
THE PROFOUND SYMMETRY OF WHICH
IS SOMEHOW PRESENT IN THE INNER STRUCTURE OF OUR INTELLECT.

~PAUL VALERY

Draw tickets to a show or concert you want to see.
Who would go with you?

Draw a chair or stool.

Really look at the lines and shadows.

Draw the first random thing you pull out of your refrigerator.

CREATIVITY IS THE PROCESS
OF HAVING ORIGINAL IDEAS
THAT HAVE VALUE.
IT IS A PROCESS; IT'S NOT RANDOM.

~KEN ROBINSON

DRAW A DRAGON.

(YOU CAN DO IT, LOOK AT A PICTURE IF YOU NEED TO)

Draw your hand or foot.

DRAW A PEANUT FROM MEMORY

(WITHOUT LOOKING AT A REAL ONE OR A PHOTO).

THEN LOOK AT ONE (OR A PHOTO) AND DRAW IT AGAIN.

NO MAN IN THE WORLD
HAS MORE COURAGE THAN THE MAN
WHO CAN STOP AFTER EATING ONE PEANUT.

~CHANNING POLLOCK

draw yourself or a
friend as a robot.

Draw a top hat.
Who is wearing it?

DRAW A FAVORITE CHRISTMAS OR HOLIDAY ORNAMENT. IS IT FROM YOUR CHILDHOOD? DO YOU STILL HAVE IT?

(MINE IS A SMALL FADED RED GLASS BALL WITH A SNOWMAN PAINTED ON IT... ONE OF MY FIRST MEMORIES IS HANGING IT ON THE TREE)

There's something about a holiday
that isn't all about how much money you spend.

~Hilarie Burton

Draw a circus or amusement park.
What's the scariest ride or attraction?
What is the most fun?

WRITE OUT THE ALPHABET (OR JUST YOUR NAME) IN A FUN WAY, LIKE BUBBLE LETTERS OR FANCY SCRIPT.

DOODLE IN AND AROUND THE LETTERS.

Draw a wine bottle or vase.

Old wood best to burn,
old wine to drink,
old friends to trust,
and old authors to read.

~Athenaeus

Draw an Owl. Hoo Hoo!

Draw a stadium full of people.
Who is on stage? Is it you?

Draw an eye. Is it human or animal? Or fantasy?

Why does the eye see a thing
more clearly in dreams
than the imagination when awake?

~Leonardo da Vinci

Draw a tear drop or water drop.

DRAW A SERIES OF GEARS ALL TURNING TOGETHER.

DRAW SOMETHING THAT REMINDS YOU OF FAMILY.

The bond that links your true family
is not one of blood,
but of respect and joy in each others life.
~Richard Bach

DRAW AN INSECT.
CAN IT FLY? IS IT BEAUTIFUL OR CREEPY?

Draw a bowling ball, baseball, or other sphere.

Look at where the highlights and shadows are, both on the ball, and on the table.

DRAW A WATER HOSE COILED UP. OR IS IT A SNAKE? EEEK!

WE'RE LIKE A GARDENER WITH A HOSE
AND OUR ATTENTION IS WATER -
WE CAN WATER FLOWERS
OR WE CAN WATER WEEDS.

~JOSH RADNOR

Draw a yo-yo.

DRAW SOME TOOLS, LIKE HAMMERS OR PLIERS.

DRAW A BASKET OF SPRING FLOWERS.

FLOWERS ALWAYS MAKE PEOPLE BETTER,
HAPPIER, AND MORE HELPFUL;
THEY ARE SUNSHINE,
FOOD AND MEDICINE FOR THE SOUL.

~LUTHER BURBANK

DRAW A SUNRISE OR SUNSET.
WHERE ARE YOU?

Draw some mountains. Are the jagged and rocky or rounded and smooth? Are they covered with snow?

Draw a dog. Is she or he big? Small? Fluffy? Short-haired?

DOGS DON'T RATIONALIZE.
THEY DON'T HOLD ANYTHING
AGAINST A PERSON. THEY DON'T
SEE THE OUTSIDE OF A HUMAN
BUT THE INSIDE OF A HUMAN.
~CESAR MILLAN

DRAW YOUR DREAM VEHICLE. IS IT A CAR OF THE FUTURE? OR SOMETHING FROM THE PAST?

DRAW A WATER BOTTLE.

IS IT PLASTIC, GLASS, OR SOMETHING ELSE?

DRAW AN APPLE THREE DIFFERENT WAYS.
(MAYBE ONE IS CUT IN HALF?)

Anyone can count the seeds in an apple,
but only God can count
the number of apples in a seed.

~Robert H. Schuller

DRAW WHAT YOU SEE (OR WANT TO SEE!) WHEN YOU WAKE UP.

DRAW A ROAD. WHERE DOES IT LEAD?

DRAW SOMEONE LAUGHING.

"LAUGHTER IS TIMELESS,
IMAGINATION HAS NO AGE,
AND DREAMS ARE FOREVER."
~WALT DISNEY

Draw a fish bowl or tank. What lives in it?

Draw something tropical. A fruit, tree, or flower?

DRAW SOMETHING THAT MAKES YOU SMILE.

A SMILE IS A CURVE THAT
SETS EVERYTHING STRAIGHT.
~PHYLLIS DILLER

DRAW A CITY SKYLINE.
DO YOU WANT TO BE THERE?

Draw a superhero.
Make him/her a mix of other superheroes, or make a brand new one!

Draw something green.

IT'S NOT EASY BEING GREEN.
-KERMIT THE FROG

Draw a child's toy.

Is it one that you remember from childhood?
Or does it belong to your child?

DRAW A HORSE OR A UNICORN.

DRAW YOUR FAVORITE FOOD(S).

Part of the secret of
a success in life is to eat
what you like and let the
food fight it out inside.

~Mark Twain

Draw an onion.

Yes, an onion. Pay attention to the veins in the skin and the shadows and highlights.

DRAW A PATH IN THE WOODS.

Draw a place that you want to visit.

I mean, Hawaii is beautiful,
but the world is full of beautiful places.
~Robert Kiyosaki

DRAW A CAT.

IS IT RESTING OR READY TO POUNCE? WHAT SHAPE IS ITS TAIL?

DRAW A DOOR.

IS IT PLAIN OR ORNATE? IS IT WOOD OR METAL OR SOMETHING ELSE? WHERE DOES IT LEAD?

DRAW A DREAM YOU'VE HAD.

*The future belongs
to those who believe
in the beauty of their dreams.*
~Eleanor Roosevelt

Draw a person or creature in the style of Anime.

(online research is okay if you need it.)

DRAW A PAPER BAG.

IS THERE ANYTHING IN IT? IS IT CRISP AND NEW, OR OLD AND WRINKLED?

DRAW A CAT'S PAW, TOP AND BOTTOM VIEW.

One small cat changes coming home
to an empty house to coming home.
~Pam Brown

DRAW A COMPUTER.

IS IT A DESKTOP OR LAPTOP? IS SOMEONE USING IT?

draw a spaceship.

Draw 4-5 different trees.

EVEN IF I KNEW THAT TOMORROW
THE WORLD WOULD GO TO PIECES,
I WOULD STILL PLANT MY APPLE TREE.

~MARTIN LUTHER

Draw a dragonfly.

DRAW A GUITAR.

DO YOU PLAY? DO YOU KNOW SOMEONE WHO DOES? MY SON PLAYS, AND I'D LOVE TO SHOW HIM YOUR DRAWINGS! SEND THEM IN!

DRAW A SELF-PORTRAIT.
(YOU KNEW IT HAD TO BE IN HERE SOMEWHERE!)

I rage against Vincent van Gogh
for needing to die at 37, after painting
for only ten years.

~Jerry Saltz

DRAW BAMBOO, EITHER ONE STALK OR A FOREST FULL.

DRAW A FRUIT THAT YOU LOVE.

draw the night sky.

And I think the violets
are little snips of the sky
that fell down when the angels
cut out holes for the starts to shine through.
~ Lucy Maud Montgomery

Draw a chain or chain links.

DRAW AN ANIMAL MADE UP OF DIFFERENT ANIMAL PARTS
(EX. A DOG'S HEAD, RABBIT EARS, GIRAFFE NECK, ZEBRA STRIPES, ETC!)

Draw a comfy couch for reading or cuddling with a pet.

MY IDEA OF ABSOLUTE HAPPINESS
IS TO BE IN BED ON A RAINY DAY,
WITH MY BLANKIE, MY CAT, AND MY DOG.
~ANNE LAMOTT

Draw a castle.
Who lives there?

Draw someone crying.

DRAW AN ARTICLE OF CLOTHING.
YOUR FAVORITE SHIRT, A SOCK, OR ANYTHING!

THE FINEST CLOTHING MADE
IS A PERSON'S OWN SKIN,
BUT, OF COURSE, SOCIETY DEMANDS
SOMETHING MORE THAN THIS.

~MARK TWAIN

DRAW YOUR FAVORITE CARTOON CHARACTER.

Draw a book, closed and open.

what book is it?

Draw how you are feeling right now.

Leave space to come back and draw a different emotion.

The artist is a receptacle for emotions
that come from all over the place:
from the sky, from the earth,
from a scrap of paper,
from a passing shape,
from a spider's web.

~ Pablo Picasso

Draw some candy.
What is your favorite?

Draw your favorite number and embellish it.
1 2 3 4 5 6 7 8 9 0

Draw a beach, ocean, lake, or river.
What animals are nearby?

I love the beach. I love the sea.
All my life I live within –
in front of the sea.
~Rafael Nadal

Draw a bunch of circles, then fill them in with doodles.

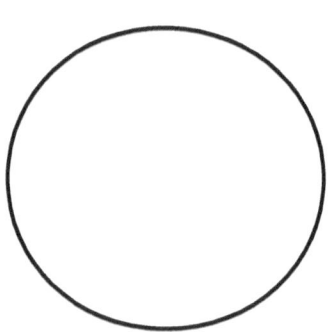

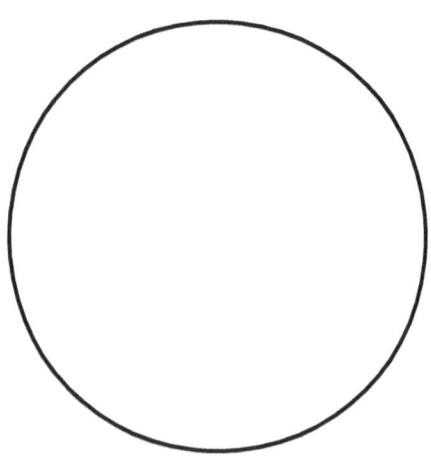

DRAW A HOUSE.

IS IT BIG OR SMALL? WHO LIVES THERE?

DRAW YOURSELF OR A FRIEND AS A CENTAUR.

FANTASY IS A NECESSARY INGREDIENT IN LIVING,
IT'S A WAY OF LOOKING AT LIFE THROUGH
THE WRONG END OF A TELESCOPE,
AND THAT ENABLES YOU TO LAUGH AT LIFE'S REALITIES.

-DR. SEUSS

Draw a turtle.

DRAW A MAZE.

DRAW ONE OF YOUR FAVORITE PAINTINGS
(MINE IS STARRY NIGHT BY VAN GOGH),
BUT MAKE IT YOUR OWN.

I often think the night
is more alive and more
richly colored than the day.
~Vincent Van Gogh

Draw an enchanted forest.
What makes it enchanted?

Draw a close up of someone's hair.
Is it curly or straight? What color is it?

DRAW A CAMERA.
IS IT OLD FASHIONED OR NEW?

Life is like photography,
we develop from the negatives.
~ unknown

Draw someone from your childhood (real or imaginary).

Draw a statue or landmark, such as the Eiffel Tower or the Statue of Liberty.

Draw a fairy sitting on a flower or mushroom.

Come away, O human child:
To the waters and the wild
with a fairy, hand in hand,
For the world's more full of
weeping than you can understand.
~William Butler Yeats

DRAW SOME POTS AND PANS.

DRAW YOUR FAVORITE DESSERT. YUM!

Draw some new sharp pencils.
Are they colored?

In spite of everything I shall rise again:
I will take up my pencil,
which I have forsaken in my great discouragement,
and I will go on with my drawing.

~Vincent Van Gogh

DRAW A FAMILY CREST.
WHAT IS IMPORTANT TO YOU AND YOUR FAMILY?

In every conceivable manner,
the family is link to our past,
bridge to our future.

~Alex Haley

Find a beautiful piece of art.
If you fall in love with Van Gogh
or Matisse or John Oliver Killens,
or if you fall love with the music of
Coltrane,
the music of Aretha Franklin,
or the music of Chopin -
find some beautiful art and admire it,
and realize that that was created
by human beings just like you,
no more human, no less.

~Maya Angelou